CW00383579

Granite Zero

Sean Thompson

The Beginning

7th March 1987 I came into the world, and to be fair even then I was never the biggest. Being born in a military hospital I was always going to be destined to join the forces at some point in my life.

I was the youngest of two, my older brother Darren has and always will be a huge part of my life, more than a brother, more like best friends. Later in life, both each other's best men at our weddings.

My Mother a fiery welsh woman with a terrible fiery temper, with a look that could kill and wouldn't back down from the biggest of men. She is my biggest supporter in life always on my side even when I don't deserve it.

My Father has always been a huge inspiration in my life, most people say I'm morphing into him each day at a time, a deep gruff voice with a bark that scares anyone. 22 years service in the military furthered to 20 years in HM Prison service.

He is my hero no matter what. From the start, family has always been a major part of my life. For the most part my Mum and Dad seemed to have a happy loving relationship, a few problems usually around drink saw me see things that a young man shouldn't see, and as much as this is an open read about my life certain things will be kept to myself.

I grew up in a small city best know for its cider, beef and the SAS. Hereford is always home to me.

Growing up, I was a mummy's boy, as much as my dad was my hero, my Mum was always the go to. And alongside her my Gran, I spent most of my childhood growing up visiting my Gran in the welsh valley's. We would spend weekends and half term's there, playing soldiers in the garden or heading up the mountains as well as down the park for a kick about. Her standard response was "Bloody kids" My Gran was the world to me, and losing her when I was 13 was difficult for me, my first real loss. Even to this day I can hear her wheezy laugh, due to the amount she smoked.

Even with the years that have past, she is firmly in my memory and always will be, I wonder if she would be proud of me what I have achieved and later how she would be with my own children. Even though I'm not religious I like to think she is looking upon me and smiling.

*

I've always been a gifted sportsman, being able to play most sports pretty well. Although I've never really excelled in one particular sport but played to a decent level in several. Sports have always been a love and passion of mine, using them to help centre myself.

My three loves of sport have always been Football, Rugby and Basketball.

I took to basketball a lot easier than the others, and even at 5ft 6 inches, I managed to play to a decent level, almost making it to the national league before deciding on my future career with the Air Force.

School life were some of the best days I had, although starting off at primary school, I was bullied, and at a young age it was difficult to roll with, being small, skinny with big ears as well as huge rat like teeth didn't work in my favour. It started with someone I thought was a friend, but I was wrong, daily I would be picked on, name calling, pushed about, this would go on for a few years, back then I struggled with confidence and had quiet low self esteem, unable to break out of the shy kid mentality, which all played perfectly into the bullies hands.

It wasn't until I started to play sports and make new friends that I began to gain confidence, football is where it first started. Playing for a local club, Tupsley Pegasus, I also got to play a year above, and that's where it started. I had to be stronger, I had to not take any shit, start sticking up for myself, even to this day I won't take any shit on the football pitch, and definitely not verse to putting in a hard tackle.

By the age of fifteen I was playing men's football, at seventeen with a number of yellows and reds to my name I was getting a rep for putting in the work and the tackles nobody else wanted to. I wasn't the most talented player by any means, but I worked hard.

I found myself losing control in a number of games, my temper getting the best of me, making horrendous decisions and even worse tackles, I always had a fire that would burst into life at the top of a hat. On the sports pitch, sometimes unable to control the frustration of losing, and my misguided temper would make me see red too many times.

My main problem with sports was that I was always willing to help the team instead of being selfish, maybe if I was more prone to sticking to one position I would have gone further, but the fact I could adapt and play multiple positions didn't often work in my favour.

At school I managed to play Rugby a year above, in football I was always playing in older teams (as I stated men's by the age of fifteen), cricket which I hated, again a year above.

As for Basketball, I had a natural talent at it, even at my height, playing men's at twelve, then by year 8, I was playing for the year 11's.

Basketball kept me focused, me and my best friend Chris, we would play day and night, until the street lights came on and even past that, we were more or less self taught. In our final year at school in Sixth

Form we part of the Hereford County team, the Hereford Hawks made up of 14-19 year olds, playing amongst the Gloucester Men's league.

It was a different and difficult task, we had the raw talent amongst our team, with no real coaching, it was difficult for us to progress.

I was known in the league as a talent, but with a bad attitude, most games I was singled out, one game in particular comes to mind.

Hereford Hawks vs Gloucester Police

"Watch that number 8"

I have never been singled out in a game as much as I had in that game, myself and Chris were the eldest in the team at Seventeen. I was targeted with each possession of the ball, Chris was targeted at each defensive play, the Referee's decision wasn't fair.

The game was on the verge of boiling point, Chris was frustrated being called out for fouls that weren't, same with myself, every drive to the hoop I was hit with no call, the game was becoming more of a fight than a basketball match, we were teenagers not men, and the bully mentality from the police was not sportsman like.

The last straw came. I Got the ball over half way, I knew my marker couldn't guard me 1 on 1, I stepped to my right as he went to block I span, around him making my way into the key, then...

SMACK ... forearm to the mouth,
I step back holding the ball, blood trickling from my mouth as my lip split on my braces....

"TRAVELLING" the ref called

"YOU HAVE TO BE FUCKING KIDDING ME REF" I shouted as I slammed the ball down... my anger and frustration boiling over

"Technical Foul" the ref ordered

"YOU'RE A FUCKING JOKE, THIS IS RIDICULOUSLY, YOU'RE KIDDING ME" I yelled out with blood pouring from my mouth.

"Second Technical you're out"

With that I was sent off, as I stormed off the court to the changing room, our coach did the same, taking all the players off and refused to play, my Dad was over at the bench of the Police team

With a raised angry voice " You should be ashamed of yourselves, they're kids, you could have beat them without this tactic, I hope you're kicked out of the league"

Over the next couple seasons we would out play and beat the Gloucester Police team.

Playing basketball with Chris was always my favourite passtime, staying up watching the All Star games, getting exited about the 2001 playoff finals between my 76ers and his Lakers, those years we shared from the age of two, meeting at playgroup to even now, thirty years on. Even now with sometimes months of not speaking and also living on opposite sides of the country, we talk like we have never been apart from each other.

I've never been academic by any means, in fact if I wasn't playing sports I really didn't care about other subjects, most teachers thought I was lazy and had a lack of focus, and to some extent they where right. Although once I got to college, I found out I was Dyslexic, which explained a lot in regards to my reading, writing, spelling etc.

Which is probably why I wanted to be more involved into physical pursuits, going through Secondary School and then College, I only had one goal in mind, that was to be like my dad, a PTI in the Royal Air

Force, I took BTEC in Sports and Exercise Science to help me on my way.

During this period my parents bought a gym in my home town of Hereford. This is where I honed my craft as a Personal Trainer, and where I first started to see my size increase. I loved every second of working there, working as a team with my brother and with a close friend of mine "the kid" Harry.

From Seventeen to Twenty, me and Harry would cause havoc, and this is where a part of my darkness would take flight.

Not sure if it's due to being bullied as a kid or if it's your typical short man syndrome, I have an awful temper, accentuated when I have a drink, countless times I was bollocked by my mum and dad over my fighting in night clubs, especially when coming home with cuts and bruises over my face and knuckles. On more than one occasion being lucky and not being picked up by the police. This type of behaviour would continue until I had my first child.

But before that time I was a nightmare, some nights I spent actually looking for a scrap, never backing down from anyone. If I wasn't trying to pull a girl, I was trying to get into a fight. To this day I still have that temper, as we would say 0 to Flash in seconds.

At Nineteen, I was still very much a boy, I'd get a girlfriend and then find a 'better one' I had a fair share of girlfriends. I had met a lady who's name I won't share, I thought she was the one, although everyone told us how we aren't meant to be, how our personalities didn't match, how she was up her own perfect arse, and how I'm still a boy.

Well these people where of course 100% right. I didn't listen, I thought I was in love, until the next chick showed me attention, but still I'd hide it, we even got engaged, she moved into my parents, then like just like that it was over. I was broken hearted, I stayed in my room for days, slouching about in my bathrobe for days, I didn't want to talk to anyone, I didn't want to eat, I didn't even want to get pissed.

I was angry, I knew she was with someone else, who could blame her, I was an asshole, not for all the relationship but a section.

I took my anger out on every one, from getting into fights on the football pitch, nights out, and also fights with the old man at home (verbally) I wasn't the boy/man I was supposed to be. I needed time, but what I needed more was to change my behaviour.

I would take the time to pick my dads brain, he had so much knowledge of the RAF, and that's what I truly wanted to do. Sitting in awe of him whilst he told me stories of his time, whilst sipping a pint. I absorbed everything he said. After that I was hooked, ever since a kid, I dreamed of wearing the uniform, almost living the life of 'Action Man' as I had spent my childhood playing with.

My Dad would say "Take a look around, the men in this bar have stories" I'd sit back nursing my pint, knowing most here were either veterans of, attached to or serving in the world famous 22 Special Air Service Regiment. Usually, they would sit and not say much, not wanting to draw attention to themselves and why should they, they had nothing to prove to others.

During a one to one chat with my Dad having a beer, I noticed my Dad giving a nod of respect behind me. Turning round and taking in the room, I noticed a man sat in the corner drinking on his own, gruff looking long handle bar moustache, I thought nothing of it turned back to my Dad.

"Who's that old boy ?!!" I asked as I questioned him regarding him. He simply replied "Now that's a man with stories, you will know one day boy" I shrugged it off with my boyish naivety, later I realised it was John McAleese, famously known for his part in the SAS Iranian Embassy Raid in 1980.

2007 I began my journey in joining the RAF, trips to Gloucester to the Armed Forces Careers Office. I had to take part in a medical, aptitude tests as well as an interview. I had missed out on PTI by one mark, slightly gutted but I desperately wanted to join the Royal Air Force and follow in the Thompson's footsteps. There were a long list of roles I could do, but one stood out to me immediately, I looked at it in its big bold letters RAF REGIMENT.

"Sean are you sure you want to choose that" I was asked, I simply replied "Yes, I want the next most physically demanding job in the Air Force"

The Twenty year old wide eyed, still wet behind the ears me didn't think to get a trade or something that will give me skills for jobs later in life. No, no I wanted guns, rifles and armoured vehicles, I wanted to be like the soldiers I had watched in the movies, I wanted to earn medals, but ultimately I wanted to be looked at with in awe.

By November, I was on my PGAC, which was my final test to see if I was fit and ready for the RAF Regiment. When I was told I passed the test, the reality of it all set in. It was about to get real very quick, that Full Metal Jacket moment of getting my head shaved and ready for basic training. A total of 32 weeks training, consisting of blood, sweat and tears awaited me.

Making the Cut

From a young age I always wanted to follow in the footsteps of my Father and Grandfather before him, both who served with pride and dignity.

With a freshly shaved number one haircut, I sat at Hereford station, waiting for the train to depart. My Mother stood with tears in her eyes and a small hit of pride in my fathers. I fought back the tears as the train made its long journey to London before getting another train to Bury St Edmunds. This is where I would call home for the next six months. I arrived the night before basic training started, that night I stayed on my own in a B&B a couple of miles from RAF Honington. Safe to say I had never felt nerves like this, all these thoughts whizzing through my mind of "Am I ready for this, am I really?" I had no idea if I really was.

On January 6th 2008, I stood and attested to serve Queen and Country. I was no longer a civilian, but a fresh faced Twenty year old, now known as AC Thompson 30044938.

We had a large training flight which consisted of sixty four of us starting on day one, I found myself in El Alimaine Flight, one of the Regiments battle honours. I remember marching out of camp, still in our suits to the nearby barbers. Just like in the movies, my hair would be buzzed off, in my eyes this was the ultimate symbol of the beginning of the process of breaking me down so they could strip us back before they started the process of rebuilding us into the military's image.

The first 4 weeks I struggled, and many times I thought of quitting and just going home, thinking "Fuck it, I'm better at my old job anyway" If it wasn't for my father and brother, I would have packed it in. The first month wasn't particularly hard, but let's just say I wasn't the best in the block. With duties such as ironing my kit and polishing boots as well as making sure my locker was exactly the same box folding as my opos. It really got me down, I felt useless and would think "Fuck, if I can't cope with the "easy" stage, then what the fuck am I going to be like when it ramps up?"

I had some long chats with some of the lads, who also backed me to stay.

Nick Anderson or otherwise known as Ginge due to his bright ginger hair, who still to this day is still one of my best friends. We would chat for hours about everything, him along with Scott Brant who was another one that kept me on track throughout training.

I had to make it to families day, this would be my first mile stone, 4 weeks in and being allowed a trip to home. It was time for a night out on the piss with my mates from home.

In true Tommo fashion I rubbed someone up the wrong way. But also in the back of my mind I knew if I fight I would have gotten into some serious shit.

The lad was laying into me with his best shots, my face looked like Brad Pitt in Fight Club, he stepped back and looked at me, my face was covered in blood and my mouth full of it, I spat blood into the mans face before saying "Is that all you got?" he walked off.

I began to walk home, "Fuck sake, my first weekend home and this, when I get back on Sunday, I'm in so much shit"

"Thompson" was all I heard

"Sir?" I replied

"What the hell happened? from what I can see, you are putting the RAF Regiment into disrepute and I'm very tempted to kick you off my course" the training wing SNCO asked.

I explained exactly what happened, and with a phone-call from my old man, which helped as I was allowed to stay on the course. With no real damage to myself physically, the real problem from the training wing SNCOs was that I didn't fight back, "Tommo why didn't you fight back? he hit you? Are you some sort of wimp?" They asked.

Looking back, I should have kicked the fuck out of that skinny runt who couldn't punch, but you live and learn.

"Thompson... what the fuck.... are these boots actually polished!" Came the question thrown at me.

"Uhhh yes, Corporal" I replied

Without a blink there went my boots as well as my locker, thinking "What the actual fuck? It's taken me over 4 weeks to finally get this right and you go and fuck it up" And for me, it's always been hard to bite my tongue. I've always found it hard trying to keep my temper in check. But watching my locker being turned upside down can push the most patient person. It was more bullshit that you just had to suck up and get on with it!

Finally, we made it to the field, learning the basics of infantry skills which would serve me well in time to come. It was something I loved and actually found myself excelling in. I loved it, being able to get out of the block, where let's face it I was dog shit. It was refreshing being able to learn the actual skills and drills that I needed to do the job.

It was during Fieldcraft, I celebrated my 21st birthday whilst out in the field at Stanta training ground! Not an ideal place or way for a young 21 year old to spend their birthday especially as there were no beers involved, but finding instead a mate bringing along and giving you a cherry Bakewell tart from the NAFFI. To this day, I haven't forgotten that small act of kindness

As each week passed I grew with confidence, looking forward to each fieldcraft from two more infantry based training fire and manoeuvre from pairs to section level, then onto one of the hardest days of my life BAYONET training, a day of beastings to the

point where you just want to explode with rage, I was
head butted by a CPL splitting my eye open, the
anger forming constantly to the point where you want
to kill, marking time on the spot shouting "KILL" at
the top of your lungs, blood pouring out, sweating
and ready to explode, it's based on controlled
aggression, seeing you worked up to boiling point
then told to stop and calm in seconds. It's what
divides the infantry soldiers from the rest. That
ability to switch from kill to chill.

Then to dig ex, living in a trench that you build
nonstop limited sleep, all there to test your ability to
cope, adapt and overcome. Then finally ex OMEGA
our final exercise, my first but not last trip to Senny
Bridge camp. Arduous terrain, huge mountains and
hills, heavy Bergans, webbing and all the ammo

needed. One of the best exercises I've ever done, we did it all, squadron level attacks, attacking and defending positions, taking trenches, hanging out, sprinting up mountains, night ambushes, to Fighting In Built Up Areas (FIBUA) whilst all camouflaged up, it brings back so many memories that I cherish every day.

Finally I made it, from almost quitting after 4 weeks, to building up and bulling my parade shoes, ready to march in front of my family with my mudguards sewn onto the shoulders of my number one jacket.

The sense of pride I had was hard to contain while standing holding my rifle at attention, seeing my mother and father smiling in the crowd, my brother holding my niece with huge smiles on their faces, Holyrood played as we marched out of the hanger.

Before we met up with our families, we stood to attention as we where given our new Squadron DZs by the Squadron WO and Squadron Leader, receiving the Snake and Dagger of 15 Squadron meant the world to me, and sharing it with so many lads I passed out with.

We started with 64 originals on basics, after weeks of hard work, we passed out with 16 originals.

Before we finally made it to the squadron, we had one more thing to pass. FIELD GUNNERS!

Becoming the Gunner

Arguably the last of the hard course, known as "THE LAST STAND" 8 weeks of advanced infantry training.

Honing and sharpening our skills, adding extra to our skill set using more weapon systems, everything from LMG, GPMG to the LAW.
The Tactical Advance to Battle (TAB's) and speed marches got longer faster as well as heavier, but at the time that didn't bother most of us, we were coming into our peak level of physical fitness.

We would spend 2 weeks at the Hythe and Lydd ranges, day in and day out, night shoots the lot, at the time it felt pointless. I just wanted to be on my bunk monging out, "Fuck sake another range, this is bollocks" I thought, but now I know I miss it, bombing up my mags 30 rounds of 5.56mm slipping them into my webbing pouch. Drilling all the stoppages drills so that they are second nature, even to this day I recall the muscle memory of hours upon hours of drills and ranges.

It's a feeling like no other, knowing that you have a piece of equipment resting in your shoulder, designed to maim and kill your fellow man, as you make ready pulling back the cocking handle, placing the round in the chamber, "At the target in front, go on" you adjust your position and make sure your sight is aligned, the image clear in your mind, gently squeezing the trigger, careful not to snatch it, so your firing position is unchanged.

You feel more than human. This is enhanced even more when you load up the 7.62mm belt fed, GPMG or otherwise known as 'The General' holding that tight to your shoulder cocking it aggressively, you have to take control of this weapon system, make it your bitch, squeeze the trigger and give out a burst of holy hell, watching and feeling the power of this weapon is like nothing you have ever felt and knowing the destruction it can cause. The smell of carbon and gun oil would fill the air.

We would be split into our different roles within the section, I was lead light pair, one of the first two in the section, the dogs, the first two would be the ones first into the action, usually short and angry and aggressive, I slotted in perfectly. Once in your pair you would have to see who was the lead. Who was the most aggressive and ready, this was between me and William Wamburu, African lad, who later became a pilot, but there was no chance this guy was going to beat me, I wanted to be number one, I smashed him, picked him up with a double leg and launched him to the ground.

We would make the long journey up to Otterburn Training ground, Newcastle way. Cold, wet and once again arduous terrain. Each day we would train and drill, we would TAB for miles with maximum weight on our backs.

We as a regiment get a lot of shit for the infamous "We have a 5 mile of death, all the scales all the bomb, we can stand toe to toe with the Paras and the Marines and say I am"

That was an understatement, the heavy weight is one thing the pace is another; mountain and hills, the unsteady ground and the 24 hour firefight at the end is what the real end ex is about. It is a lot more than just 5 miles, trust me.

It rained, boy did it rain, was supposed to be summer and it pissed it down almost every day for the whole 3 weeks, and when it finally got dry and the sun came out. It was time to practice river crossings. "Hey DS fuck you" You would try and dry out your socks in the "drying room" which basically turned into a steam room, I discovered that if you shove your socks to the bottom of your sleeping bag they will eventually dry out due to the body heat generated.

"Pass on the message" I said whilst kneeling in silence, I literally have no idea what this scouse bastard is saying.

"Oi you dickhead, what's your name" said in the scouse whisper

"Me flight?!" I answered

"You're the only dickhead I can see" he replied without thinking about his response

"Thompson Flight" I replied

"Tommo, can you hear me now?!" Came the next question

"Yes Flight" bit confused here, I know something is about to happen though.

"See that river over there.. go put your fucking head in it, wash your fucking massive ears out you cunt, then pass the fucking message on" came the reply in a nonplussed response

I had to guess what the fuck this scouse nutter was on about but luckily I got it. But for fuck sake I was actually dry.

The next time I spoke with Flight Sergeant 'Scouse' Taylor, the man behind the 5 mile of Death, would be a positive one and full of praise.

The build up to the final exercise, we had a long Speed March (more than 5 miles) I recall the pace being exceptionally fast, to the point where all sections became one giant gaggle of Gunners, a number dropped back and out of the march, but that being said you can't just let their weapon and ammo go to the wagon, distributed between the second! Fuck me, my kit was heavy, the lactic acid forming in my muscles burning, I would have given anything for the pain to stop, but I couldn't, I couldn't stop I couldn't quit absolutely, I would hate to look like a cunt in the eyes of the DS. Having your battle buddy's passing you attempting to encourage you up the mountain, as you gasp for oxygen " Fuck You!"

The final exercise was a tough live firing range, again a long TAB and straight into battle drills and fire fights for over 24hours. Zero time to chill and switch off and rest, there was no time for that, wave after wave of attacks, we had a real time man down where our CPL snapped his ankle literally seconds after I said "watch your footing"

I was amazing at taking positions, throwing grenades,

this is truly what I wanted to do.

And I was good at it.

"STOP STOP STOP" endex was called time to go

back and chill.

Until we finished off with comms training (little did I

know this wouldn't be the last) and other NVQ work.

During this time it was a strange period, I

met a girl before joining the Air Force and which we

slept together a number of times before I told her I

wanted to focus on my new career and that my mind

needed to be on that.

Little did I know my life was almost flipped upside down.

During the range package I had a phone call from the girl saying I was going to be a dad. Fuck I was scared, petrified if I'm truly honest, I didn't even like the girl that much, as harsh as it sounds I only wanted to fuck her. But after the baby was born I made the trip to Exeter to see them, see what I thought was my daughter Isabella, two long weeks learning how to change nappies, nurture and care for a tiny little girl, I fell in love with that little angel. We took a DNA test, and the results where in! I felt like I was on Jeremy Kyle. You are not the father.

An over whelming sense of relief came over me. I didn't want to be part of that family, I was only there for the baby. Soon as I knew, I was gone.

"Are you going to stay with me and bring up the baby?" She asked

"Am I fuck, I'm out" was my blunt reply

"Tommo, check this bird out!!!" a voice boomed out. I peered over Ginge's shoulder at a profile on Facebook.

"Who's that?" I quickly asked, "That's shippers new birds best mate Kate, alright ain't she, supposed to be coming up on Friday for a block party" Ginge replied

"Yeah she's alright like" I didn't want to come across to transparent but I thought fuck she's fit. And me being a sneaky fucker, I was straight on Facebook to add her, Katie Stannard, and as they say these days I slide into the DMs!

We would talk day in and day out. Exchanging numbers, deep down I was so exited that we would finally meet at the party! But Kate fell ill and couldn't come up I was gutted, so I threw it out!

"Come up on your day off, I'll meet you" I asked her. We agreed to meet at Kings Cross Station in London, and on that day my life would change for the better forever.

It was though time stopped, and there was nobody else in the packed train terminal, just her, Striking platinum hair, tight black jeans and leather jacket, lip glossed lips and my heart was pounding.

"She is incredible" I thought as my mind was racing. And as soon as our lips met for that first kiss in the middle of Kings Cross Station I knew she was the one, even if I hid it for a few weeks. The times we spent were the best, and I had to brace her for what was coming. Before the intense training, we got to have Christmas together, and this would be a Christmas like no other.

Spending Christmas Eve out having a good time in the "premier" night club in Hereford 'Dusk'. Known for its extremely rank carpets that you get stuck to, taking after the world famous Crystal Rooms.

During this time Darren was going through a very difficult period, a tough break up from his daughters mother, which caused a lot of underlining issues. Outside the club, a few choice words between people outside and a scuffle ensued, with Darren ending up in full mount, dropping fists on the lads face, I attempt to step in to stop it, (for the first time ever I was clear minded and wanted to stop the fight) I grabbed Darren to get him off the lad....

SMACK!!!!!!!!!! I was hit to the floor, I stood up, groggy. Unable to open my eye. Two lads sprinting down the road. Darren rolling on the floor with a Police officer.

"WHAT THE FUCK" I was confused at what just happened.

"It's Christmas Eve and I'm deploying to Iraq in February, I cant handle this shit"
Luckily the police officer understood and let us go.

The main bollocking would come in the morning from my Mam. I then spent the Christmas morning in AE getting my eye and eye socket checked out to make sure nothing was broken. Fortunately the eye was ok just a lot of swollen tissue, the socked had a minor fracture.

Explaining to my Mam, Dad and Katie that this time, it wasn't my fault. This was by no means the Christmas I wanted, but it turned out to be an absolute shit sandwich.

First was pre-deployment as Iraq was around the corner. Pre-deployment training started slow, with a few range packages, refresher training on comms equipment ECM and weapon systems. All the usual drills. I was selected to spend a week on advanced medic training also known as battlefield medic BFA. I loved it. Well apart from the jumped up GUIN sargent (non infantry airforce) who I refused to come to attention for, the first of many times through my military career that I couldn't hold my tongue

"Aren't you supposed to come to attention for NCOs?" He asked followed by a pause that seemed a life time. I knew I shouldn't but fuck it "I don't come to attention for GUINS" I replied, sometimes I wish I had a filter.

As the weeks progressed into months, the training got more advanced, tactics, live firing, section to squadron battle drills. Op Dalton drills to look and find IEDs. Heli drills, mount and dismount from vehicles. And the best public order training. (in case of riots) but during this part of the training, simply put this was an opportunity for the Flight vs Flight rivalry to go over board. It was like a scene from a football hooligan movie, we would attempt and some what succeed in beating the fuck out of each team, I was in my element, I lived for a scrap, I broke someone's nose, smashed a visor, and well got a bit of a pasting myself when I broke the line and got kicked the fuck out of with batons.

We were finally ready! Trained up, fighting fit, and itching to go, but at the same time….. petrified.

We where due to leave early hours of the morning, Katie stayed with me as long as she could, before I walked her to the guard room where her Mum and Dad were waiting to pick her up. I fought back the tears, in my fresh out of the packet desert cammos. The hug seemed like forever, and the kiss would stay with me the whole tour. The sinking feeling in my stomach as she got in the car was dreadful, now shes gone it's time to switch focus, count down to Iraq starts now. Few hours and we will be waiting at RAF Brize Norton, ready to fly to the desert.

Last time I was here I was a baby, this was the base my old man spent most of his lofty career as a PJI at the number one jump school. But I was here for a different reason, walking in was weird, didn't feel like any other RAF base, but like an actual Airport, most people think you fly straight to the destination. If I'm honest I did seeing movies like Jarhead, but we don't we fly to a holding base in Dubai before taking the next flight to Basra.

We flew over on the old faithful, the C130 which is also know as the Hercules. Honestly it was one of the most uncomfortable journeys I have ever taken. The noise cancelled out the music from your headphones, very little room with the amount of troops next to you, and the anxious nerves that would course through your veins, letting that you are know that you're entering a war zone. Welcome to Iraq, the lights went out! Almost time to land....

Iraq Telic 13
Last foot on the ground

The first thing that hits you when you step off the plane is the heat, it's like a warm blanket wrapped around your face. The dust in the air is clinging on your fresh unpackaged uniform, the dust surrounds you while you're standing there like a fresh new recruit waiting for orders. No one wants to speak, your in a war zone, what next?

21 years old, standing in desert Cammies scared of your life. Most will think your just in the Air Force, you're not a front line paratrooper, just the regiment Gunner with a reputation that most take to heart and think "These lot think they are infantry, but really they're just a shower of shite"

Most regiment gunners are quiet, they don't talk a lot of shit and happy with the skills they have acquired in the long vigorous training.

I've always been proud of my achievements and of my regiment, knowing what we do is a hard and well executed job. Feel free to mock and curse me but I will always be a RAF regiment GUNNER.

Operation Telic 13 was my first operational tour of duty to Iraq, we arrived in Basra on a C130 which landed with a hot landing, which made my stomach go and I remember thinking "I've just got here, I hope we don't crash"

Next was a series of briefs on ranges and other training as well as acclimatisation to the desert. Actions on rocket actions, small-arms actions, not washing you dick properly, actions on welfare issues and a whole lot more. Most of which goes in one ear and out the other, as you're just itching to get out on the ground, get some dust and sand on your uniform. I was a member of B Flight 15 Squadron Royal Air Force Regiment, we were taking over from 51 Squadron A Flight RAF Regiment. We planned for a six month tour, but it was shortened to four due to the extraction of British forces in Iraq. Our mission was to protect the Tesseral footprint so that aircraft can take off and land, subsequently to conduct outer perimeter defence of the airbase. We also conducted foot patrols in villages and also helped prevent rocket attacks on Basra airbase.

The first time you hear the rocket alarm, you shit your pants. You think "Fuck I hope this doesn't land on this tent and blow the shit out of me, I haven't even been out on the ground yet"

I was in a small tent alongside my best friend Nick Anderson that was used for accessing the Internet when the alarm went off. We stopped for a second and thought "This is got a be a drill" until the loud bangs were heard and felt the ground shake with the impact. We hit the deck and headed underneath the table that held the computers. Nervous that the bombardment would continue, it seemed to last forever. This only happens after the first time, every time after that, you carry on as normal as though it was a normal part of the day. The Americans still shit themselves, jumping outdoors, rolling around on the floor. I just sat and waited thinking "If it hits the tent, well I'm fucked anyway"

We didn't know this at the time but we would be the "last foot on the ground" we would closing up Basra air base and handing it over to US Army.

I was part of B Flight, as flights go, we where very close, switched on and decent at our job. We where attached with a few oggies (auxiliary) gunners, most were sound but there's always one absolute fuck up, the Private Pile sort from Full Metal Jacket. We had one, but to this day I don't know how he managed to get on the tour, when other respected decent gunners where left back on the rear party.

We lived in a large tent, enough for the whole flight, each had a bed space made up of bricks sandbags, iron frame and a mattress. Commonly know as a coffin, pretty apt really as if we was hit with a rocket, we would be fucked.

Most nights I would look up at the roof of my coffin, pictures of Kate scattered around the metal, my rifle at the foot of my mattress, it was like being in captivity, not knowing what the fuck was going on. But as the days went on you learned to bottle up the emotions inside and just tell everyone "Gen I'm fine, everything is good here" what a load of old shit, you just want to be at home, but this is what you signed up for, Queen and country, your duty and in reality you fucking loved it.

We worked through what seems a never ending cycle, of patrols, tesserals, compound duty, IRT, and the occasional 12 hours stand down. But the days seem to blend into each other not knowing when one ends and the other begins.

In the middle of the turn around, getting those 12 hours to sort out the well needed admin, is always greeted with high moral. Do some washing, go to the PX, send some emails or a letter, give the balls a little tickle, all helps spruce up the mood.

In the middle of the chaos is when you find the most peace. Standing on stag out in the harsh ground of the Iraqi desert, you capture moments that most will miss. As the sun rises and sparkles across the lake, absolutely still, no noise. The quietness that surrounds around you, the million thoughts running through your mind can be as chaotic as the environment that surrounds you. "How can this beautiful sight be amongst the worst place in the world?" Scanning around the area through my SUSAT on my rifle, watching the ebb and flow of the night whilst my mind is waiting and watching across this barren land.

Its amazing that we are here, in a "WARZONE" driving through in our armoured vehicles, into small villages with our weapons loaded. Everything from 5.56mm rifles to .50cal heavy machine guns, we patrolled the villages and would engage with the locals, they wanted us to stay, its not what the media and movies portray. They liked us there, keeping them safe, forcing out the bad and enforcing the good.

The villages are exactly how you would picture it, mud huts animals roaming around, barbed wire around their gardens, kids running around care free, tatty old worn out clothes always asking for chocolate and pens, "Mr, give me chocolate" most the time you give in but you just want to say " fuck off you little shit". But you know that's the limit of their English and if we are honest, most of us couldn't be arsed to learn any Arabic accept the easy stuff, "As-salamu alaykum" and "Shukran" for hello and thank you. Lets be honest here it's a fucking hard language.

Even through unpopular opinion, the RAF Regiment did patrol outside the wire, conduct missions within villages. And on this particular occasion I was part of the Sgt multiple going through a village code named CASINO, while the OC and his multiple with my best friend Nick "Ginge" Anderson and a few others were conducting the foot patrol through the village engaging with the locals. I was satelliting in the "gardens" filled with thick mud, buffalos, razor wire, and a god awful smell, a smell that would stay with us back on camp, we were later informed that we were walking through where they dumped their shit, not just rubbish but actual human shit. Its crazy that even in 2009 they didn't have a proper sewage works to get rid of the human waste from their houses, its as though we were back in time.

During our time in Iraq we would conduct many patrols withing armoured track vehicles known as the "bulldog", brilliant to manoeuvre on roads, wouldn't say they where particularly well designed for the desert, prone to getting stuck in thick Iraqi mud when it rained heavily, air conditioning was non existent. Many times I found my self sitting on top of the bulldog waiting for someone to tow us out of the thick mud.

At times without even knowing, the engine would stall and cut out, most the time it was brushed off and restarted without us even realising what had happened, your senses are pretty nullified sat in the back with one window.

Moving up the bank into the village, the bulldog began to struggle, the feeling of the engine forcing its way up but unable to make it;
First attempt failed, second attempt failed, third attempt ………. Stalled, the bulldog began to slide back, down towards the ever encroaching river, the driver really putting in the work to get the engine started, and then to all our shock as we get closer to the rivers edge…

"EVERY MAN FOR THEMSLEVES" the vehicle commander shouted as he jumped out of the rolling bulldog, leaving the driver attempting to fix the problem and 6 gunners in the back not knowing what the fuck was going on.

Inches, inches away from sinking and potentially drowning in the Iraqi water, this wasn't the first time this Sergeant would make huge errors in judgement during my time on 15 Sqn. Luckily for us, the driver fixed the problem just before we got to the waters edge. Us gunners in the back literally had no clue what the fuck was going on or what the fuck just happened until we got back to camp.

You build friendships that last a lifetime, especially on tour, with the same group of men, day in and day out, 24 hours a day for 4-6months. But let's face it, you can't always get along, frustrations build and the 0-flash becomes seconds. There are lads you never really chat with but from time to time you find yourself stagging on with them for hours on end, normally you wouldn't give them the time of day but "hey" got nothing else to chat about. There was one lad, an oggie, who struggled, was picked on by most of the flight because of the way he was. There were lads left behind on the rear party that should have been out there but we got stuck with him. He was thick as mince, but chatting and actually getting to know him a little more there was definitely severe learning difficulties going on. Most of the lads though were switched on, good guys, that were highly trained and capable, we were itching to get some action.

We would have heightened senses each time we went out, especially when the weather would turn, a yellow mist of dust would cut through your visibility making it more difficult to see anything even 5m next to you. This was when we were most vulnerable, the enemy wasn't stupid they knew that when the weather turned was the optimal time to place IEDs. It's mad to think at the age of 22, I could walk out on each patrol and risk life and limb for people at home I'd have never met, and never will.

We would get opportunities to be attached to the sniper section, help carry out patrols with them, during the night hours, moving undetected, in and around vulnerable points to ensure the safety other the other flights and also conduct surveillance missions on villages gathering intelligence. There were six of us, four snipers and myself as well as another called Willow, to make up the numbers carrying the ECM. We were on the outskirts of one of the villages, on the way to a high threat area to conduct a surveillance op.

Scattered on the ground were girls underwear, all over the floor, small bras, pants, you name it. "Willow, mate this isn't right?" after saying that, out of one of the houses, noises where heard, uncomfortable screams, mixed with laughter and cheering, cries, and peering through my sight I could see 3 small girls and boys being raped by a group of males. My blood was boiling I wanted to cock my rifle and end those sick fucks lives, take them out one by one. To which I was quickly informed by the section commander "Tommo, this isn't our mission, that is not our fight, they cant know we are here, we are to observe and report, that is all "Ah, fuck you I want to slaughter them" but all that comes out of my mouth is "Yeah, roger that"

Iraq for me was an eye opener, seeing how these people are, how they live their culture, how different they are to us back home in the UK. All the kids have ever grown up with, are men in uniform driving in and out of their homes and villages with huge machine guns. To them its just life, how things are. For me, it wasn't action filled like the movies, I wasn't shot at, on a daily basis, rocket attacks became the norm but that was just part of the experience, I didn't think I had the trauma or the stress that others have had in the past. But this was just tour one.

15 Squadron RAF Regiment ended up being the last British force on the ground in Basra, I was out in the tesseral foot print, watching others from the British military leaving to go to Cyprus, I watched on the top of a Mastiff armoured vehicle, my rifle next to me, and a cigar lit in my mouth, puffing out the smoke, I turned to Ginge and said, "We did it Kid" taking

another hit of the cigar "Let's enjoy this victory dance"

The doors of the hanger began to open slowly, to the sound of cheering, familiar faces dotted around the hanger, but my eyes were locked and fixed on one person and one person only.

Katie.

I didn't even realise that her friend that had given her a lift to the base was even there, four months apart, four long months. I had missed her like mad, I knew she was the one, she stuck by me through this period, her boyfriend deploying to war and was still there when I came home. At that moment, I knew no matter what life threw at us we could manage.

The next few weeks I didn't know what to do with myself, I was still on edge, and checking around the car every time I got out, was unable to fully switch off completely and relax. I found myself filling my days by drinking, starting with a pint here, pint there, several watching the ashes…. I don't even like cricket, I had really lost something, I wanted to go back, but I didn't know why.

Once again, this time as a Squadron we marched into the hanger, this time it was full with friends, family, loved ones and some high ranking officers. We stood to attention, I could see my Dad and Mam beaming with pride as the station commander walked passed each of us handing out our operation medals for Telic 13. I have never had a sense of pride like it, the thought that I have truly accomplished something, I was literally living the dream, the dream that I had as a boy, this medal will look amazing mounted on my number 1 dress. I wanted more.

She Said Yes

I was a bag of nerves all day. I went to Maidstone town centre and was pacing around all day and afternoon. I had booked the restaurant, nice rustic restaurant, decent food and drink. Next was to get the ring. It had to be perfect, it had to be just right. Katie had very small delicate fingers, never wore gold, but needed a metal that wouldn't lose its shine with all the bleaching, washing and day to day wear and tear. I stood at the window of the jewellers for what seemed like hours, checking out each ring four or five times maybe more. "It's got to be perfect" I thought as I entered the shop, it was like flies around shit. "Can I help you sir.....do you need assistance" I was asked as I entered the shop, "Fucking hell mate, of course I do!" Luckily for me one of Katies friends was working (cheeky discount for me) We spent a lifetime weighing up the right ring, the right metal, the shape of the diamond down to the last detail. It was perfect, she will love it, she deserved the best.

Katie is one of the least materialistic people I know, she also has a heart of gold, puts everyone before herself, its endearing and a trait I always wish I had. She deserves the best that I could afford and give without doubt.

Still the nerves shot through me.. "What if she says no? …. What if her dad say no?? …. What if you make a tit of yourself… Mate you know she hates surprises and being centre of attention. I'm doing this, get a grip Tommo"

Check list :

✓ *Restaurant booked (done)*

✓ *Ring bought (done)*

✓ *New outfit complete with rascal leather looking jeans (didn't know they did until I wore them) (done)*

✓ *Hair sorted (done)*

• *Ask potential father in laws permission….*

Fuck!!

I walked into the living room, twitchy, anxious I could see Mark (Kate's Dad) and Alison (Kate's Mum) in the dining room. (lets do this) "Mark, Alison…….Is this (I said as I pulled out the box and put it on the table with the lid open)" Mark began to giggle like a child. "YESSSSS .." Mark said with a stupid grin on his face. "Ring good enough for your daughter?" I said in a strong confident voice. Alison smiled with a hint of a tear in her eye. Mark though on the other had continued to giggle "You said ring" Fuck sake, I was a bag of nerves, but in fairness this helped me calm myself down "Of course it is" Alison said with a smile.

As we were dropped off at the Whelden Hall, I was so nervous, but I would like to think I hid it well, although like a dick I didn't change the box, the fucking thing was digging so hard into my thigh, the pain of that and the nerves were making me so anxious... I must have left to use the toilet at least 4-5 times, that was before even the main course arrived.

Katie was looking as stunning as ever, her giant eyes sparkling, "She knew…she must know" I thought, I'm not usually so fidgety. I got up one last time spoke with the waitress, "I'm about to propose, could you get some champagne ready please? Oh and the desert menu"

I calmly walked back towards my seat, outside I was as cool as a cucumber, inside my heart was racing. The ring box in my hand, down I went. Took Katie's hand and looked up into those big beautiful eyes "Katie Louise Stannard…. Will you do me the honour of being my wife?" I asked, that look of shock on her face and the pause that literally felt like a second, actually felt like a lifetime. "Yes" (course it was a yes, never a doubt). The ecstatic feeling stayed with us for the rest of the night.

The Squadron was getting ready to deploy once again, this time to Kandahar, Afghanistan. Before the pre-deployment started to ramp up, I spent as much time as I could with Katie.

She fell pregnant, unfortunately we lost it pretty quickly. Katie was pretty heart broken, I seemed to block this out at first. Then Katie fell pregnant once again, this time it was twins. We were over the moon. Twins my god what if it's two boys, what if it's girls, or one of each, I was ecstatic, elated with the news.

We both made the mistake to let friends and family know too early. You might say we put the bad luck on ourselves. I've never seen Katie in so much pain, all day and most of the night in agony. I drove her to Bury St Edmunds hospital, where we were told we had lost one of the twins. A few days later I took Kate to Kings Hill private medical practice where we were told we had lost the second, there was no heartbeat. I took Kate back to her Mum and Dads, we barely said a word, her brother's were in the kitchen. Kate went straight to her room to be on her own.

I spoke to her brothers and explained what had happened and that she might need some space but also will need a lot of love. I walked out of the house, sat in the car in total silence. And sobbed, I had lost 3 babies, what if we can't have kids, tears streaming down my face. I was devastated. But had to be brave for kate, she needs the support more than I do.

I was back at it, range packages, medic training, comms training, live field firing and OP Barma (new IED drills) spend weeks on end away from Kate, training, training and more training. I was able to take the most of the weekends off or the odd week off that I was given.

We were getting closer and closer to deploying when we found out the news.
8 weeks, then 12 weeks still there, almost completely safe. I WAS GOING TO BE A DAD!!.

As amazing as that sounds, I had to focus on the task in hand, in a matter of weeks I would be flying to the desert again. It was hard enough the first time with just a girlfriend, but now it's a fiancé and my unborn child.

The lads would joke that now I was up on the Deadpool list, seeing as I have so much to lose, it would be me first to step on an IED or be shot. Squaddie humour aye. Cunts.

Jokes aside, now 23 years old sat writing a letter to my future wife and unborn child incase the worst would to happen, tears rolling down my cheeks at the thought of not coming home, and someone else raising my child that I never met. Would she know her daddy was a hero, that he selflessly put himself in harms way so that others could have the freedoms we enjoy at home.

It's hard writing a letter! Its hard to remain focused, a distracted Gunner is a dead gunner.

This time I was holding so tight, I didn't want to let go, I hated this part of the tour, being out there when you have things to take your mind off what's happening at home, but this moment, time seemed to speed up. I would kneel down and kiss Kate's bump. I whispered "Don't worry daddy will be home soon" I looked at Kate and tell her "Not to cry, I'll be home before you know it" I would kiss her one last time, holding back my own tears and step on to the coach and set off back to RAF Brize Norton

OP HERRICK 13

3 Miles Up, 3 Miles Down

Whoever said they're not scared is a liar,
Afghanistan is a different animal. Most of us had
been to Iraq and thought we were biggy big bollocks
rocking around. Afghanistan made the Iraq tour look
like a lads holiday. We went out with 51 Squadron
for some familiarisation of the ground, the villages in
amongst the barren wasteland that we would call
home for the next few months. Endless desert fields,
in the distance FOB Luke, underneath the large
mountain that could be seen for miles and miles,
known as 3 mile mountain. What sticks with you
most is the smell, which can only be described as shit.
Unfortunately for the RAF Regiment the main
compound at Kandahar air base was next to the
camp sewage works aka "POO POND" it's a smell
that will stay with me for ever.

Wasn't long into the tour that we would be called in and told that we would be handing KAF to the Americans, so having around 100 or so RAF Regiment gunners conduct patrols, tesserals to protect almost 30,000 ISAF forces on camp, once again a lot of shit is thrown at the Regiment for not going out of the wire. I'm sure they slept well on camp knowing we was doing our jobs, fucking REMF's.

Moving around the different areas of Kandahar brought some amazing sights, in the south looking out into the Red Desert, rolling red sand dunes of luscious sand, with a few Kutchi camps (nomads) couldn't believe what I was looking at, it was as if I was on the set of Star Wars. Out in the west setting up a Zulu muster, stepping out and looking at the vast open desert, again so quiet so peaceful, you wouldn't believe that you were in a war zone. I could hear the distinctive call to prayer echoing around for miles away. At night you can look up and see every star in the sky, it was beautiful, peace within the chaos. The ground was so flat, KAF was lit up like a Christmas tree, an insurgence wet dream for setting off rocket attacks towards the camp.

It wasn't long before we got a glimpse of the real Afghanistan. Routine patrols and the lead Jackal spotted a group of fighting age males, digging within a potential VP, confirmed by the commander of the Panther, using the thermal imaging camera. Huge red flags, potential IED team, we kept eyes on them and their movements, while I radioed through all the information and awaited orders to detain. While the confirmation came in, we searched the males, and used X spray (explosive detector) "Boss, its positive…. They have explosives all over their hands" bag and tag lets get these fuckers to the detention centre.

"Tommo you're going with them" this meant that it would be a nice trip with these locals to Camp Bastion for them to be questioned in relation to connection to other IED's placed and other teams.

Sitting opposite them as we loaded them onto the C130 was amazing, sat with blindfolds on their heads, zip ties on their wrists, shaking like shitting dogs as the propellers began to warm up and the aircraft took off, smiling to myself as I knew new they had no idea what was to come.

We landed at Camp Bastion in Helmand province, we were taken to varsity for them to be questioned. I felt pretty smug, until it was my turn to sit in the hot seat. Not knowing I was going to be questioned in the detaining of these males. I was sat in the middle of the room, army Captain in front of me, the right, left and rear of me were special forces operators, with their long hair, magnificent beards, RAB jackets, plucking the information out of me. The nerves coursing through my veins at this moment. I felt as though I was in the wrong, they pulled apart what happened with a fine tooth comb.

"Sorry, SAC Thompson, is it…" I was asked.

"Yes sir" I replied

"Right, I understand why you're here as the arresting soldier, but where the fuck is your witness, everything you are saying, you done all the right drills, but without the witness it's worthless, pointless, who's your boss? Why didn't he send a witness with you?" Came the flurry of questions from the officer in front of me.

I was in a state of shock and felt like an absolute knob head, no wonder we get shit from so many units, shit drills.

This was the first Christmas I'd spend away, and I couldn't be further away, but with anything, you have to take some sort of positive, a happy moment that will always be with you, I was given an early Christmas present.

I wish I was there when Katie found out, but the phone call made me ecstatic, it had been a hard few weeks. Eight days on the ground, back in resupply and back out. So sat using the Sat phone I managed to get a spare 5 mins to make a phone call, when Katie told me I was going to have a daughter, I was over the moon, we had tried so hard to fall pregnant and now I'm going to be a dad of a beautiful angel, and join the 'Daddies with pretty daughters hunting club'

The temperature drops to below -5c at night, the cold of the desert really stays with you, sleeping in the middle of a Zulu muster, unzipping your sleeping bag, seeing the clear night sky, and the frost forming on your bag. No matter what, you can't take away the untold beauties that the desert holds. It really does relax you and helps to reset the mind, you really need it especially with the lack of sleep, patrol after patrol, and sprog gobshites getting too big for their boots, it sends even the calmest people into flash point. As for me I'm always at a higher level anyway, so not doing a simple task like gathering the mail for the lads to get some moral is going to end with my forehead on your nose.

Christmas this year was like no other, you make it as festive as possible, but there is only so much you can do in a desert, a Christmas hat, maybe a small tree, might even get 5 mins to make a phone call or tickle your balls before being back on the ground. One thing we did have was Christmas diner, hands down the worst, but we made the most of it the best we could, that night out on the ground looking out with Dan Shipper and Liam Clarke. Two lads that I went through basic training with, Dan now married to Katies best friend and lives very close, we where chewing the fat as we did most the time, lighting a cigar and blowing out the smoke into the freezing Afghanistan air thinking this isn't so bad.

This tour wasn't without some scares though, for me I would flutter between being the OP Barma commander and being part of the actual search team. And one time has stuck with me to this day. "Stop, Stop, Stop, guys I think I have something" I conducted the drills so that I could get down on my belt buckle to check the area, to which an exposed wire I could see. "Just confirming guys I can see a wire" as I started my drills I got "Tommo, hurry up, we are in Kandahar not Helmand it's nothing"

I ignored the comment because I'm not rushing this, like fuck I am. Next thing I see the commander making his way over, stood over the top of me, sees the exposed wire..... places his hand on it..... and pulls it out.

Time stood still, seemed like an eternity. My arsehole was going 5p 50p and my heart was racing as fast. I thought that was it, we would have both been blown up. I had my eyes closed shitting myself. Then a kick to the helmet, "See, fucking told you Tommo, now stop being a cunt and move on" I was still in a state of shock, wasn't for a few moments later that it sank in, "That cunt could have killed me" I was fuming, few days later he was moved to a different flight.

One of the Lads managed to get some vodka smuggled in, where I managed to get some whiskey in , thanks to Katie, although it did have a hint of soap to the flavour. We watched 2010 become 2011 which would be one of the best years of my life. We smoked a cigar, and drank whiskey like we were at home.

For the most part this tour was pretty easy, in regards to kinetic action, but we felt we were doing the job we needed to do, hearts and minds with the locals, going out giving them items like blankets, radios etc. But that doesn't mean the threat wasn't real. And that was always in the back of your mind, you can't relax at any moment because it can all change in a blink of an eye.

"Troops, threat warning, keep an eye out for locals on mopeds, they are turning them into a Vehicle Improvised Explosive Device (VIED)

Most of us looked at each other, do these dickheads know how many mopeds are cutting about out on the ground, part from fucking Toyota Hilux's, that's all they drive. Standing at the front of a snap Vehicle Check Point (VCP) As the lead searcher, I had a decent top cover watching over.

Traveling at speed, I could see a moped in the distance.

"Tommo, got a moped coming in at speed" came the message loud and clear.

"Yeah, seen roger that I'll stop and search" I replied. As I finished the call over the PRR, I raised my right hand to signal the stop…. (nothing) I squared my position, raised my hand and shouted "STOP!" But nothing, the moped continued at speed and getting closer.

Crazy thoughts running through my mind, I grabbed the handle of my pistol, pulled it out of the hosteler, raised it up, pointing it at the speeding local, (still nothing) cocked my pistol, my heart beginning to race, red flare popped by the top cover, but nothing, they were still traveling at speed towards the VCP

BANG!!!

I fire, the round scuffing the ground in front of the traveling moped, the local began to wave his arm to signal, and slams his feet into the floor and begins to skid towards the VCP. I approached the moped, my pistol pointing at the local, he was old, grey, dirty and toothless, wearing dusty filthy clothes. Smiling at me, I speak to the terp, my pistol firmly pointing at the locals head, "Ask this fuck stick why he didn't stop!!!!" I shouted, pissed off that he had put us all in harms way and potentially having to apply lethal force. The Terp translated to the locals amusement, and got a reply in Arabic. The Terp turned to me and explained "His breaks don't work"

You got to be kidding me, I replied "Tell him, he was almost shot" we proceeded with the search, and let him on his way.

Its moments like that, you can sit back and laugh about after, but during that moment, the adrenaline rushing through your veins makes everything slow down, what was only a few seconds felt like an hour.

Being on QRF was always good, literally waiting for something to happen, getting little downtime which consisted of hitting the gym and playing on the PlayStation. One night, I managed to get away to get some moral and to make a phone call home. Sat in a phone booth listening to everything Katie had to say...

"OooooooWooooooo "Rocket ATTACK"

"Fuck" I said, trying not to let Katie hear it and panic. "What's that?!!" Katie asked extremely worried.

"Umm" was all I could muster as there was a huge bang on the door "Tommo move now" was all I heard. Soon as the QRF commander said that the phones went dead.

The rockets hit the camp, missing the RFS compound but only just, unfortunately hitting the Estonian accommodation block and lives where lost.

We deployed rapidly, getting out on the ground to search the POO (point of origin) sometimes the insurgents would remain in situ to watch their handy work. Others flee, usually leaving some nice presents for us to find. This time we found nothing, just scorch marks from where the rockets had been fired from.

A huge sense of disappointment would come over the lads, we wanted to catch these guys, we wanted the chance to put rounds down!

But once again another time where adrenaline is pumping, ready to get exited then nothing, just a dump of adrenaline and a lot of rage, anger and clearing of excitement just left with a meh feeling. It's emotions like that which are the hardest to process. Not knowing whether you are coming or going.

Life in Kandahar was pretty decent, we spent days in the Forward Operating Base known as FOB Luke, named after a fallen gunner from a tour before.

Front of the FOB was the main gate and facing the Air Base. To the left was the accommodation block, a few tents, the mess room, gym and final was the

mortar pit.

Rear of the FOB were the stores, med tent and the

shitter, to the right were the American contractors

that controlled the balloon, which observed the entire

Area of Operations (AO)

The towers that provided overwatch into different

areas, front was towards the closest village, armed

with the General, otherwise known as the big

powerful sexy GPMG, the other tower equally armed

with your own individual weapon systems, mine

being a L85 A2 with (Underslung Grenade Launcher

(UGL) or Betty as I called her.

The rear tower, the worst, facing the giant 3 mile mountain. Looking directly towards it.

During your time in the tower, it gives you a chance to think, and once again having amazing picturesque views, especially during sunrise and sunsets, looking out to the vast areas of villages and hearing the call to prayer which bellowed out. The morning dew and mist rising up from the ground after the freezing winter nights, again the feeling of such peace. So calm so quiet!

Towards the end of the tour, the weather took a turn for the worst, all we had was torrential rain, constant pouring from the sky. The roads in and out of the villages just turned to mush, foot patrols became something out of a Benny Hill sketch, constantly slipping on your ass, which when wearing at least 90lbs of kit, maybe more wasn't fun smashing into the floor, snapping kit, rolling ankles, it just fucked you off.

The Handover to the US Army 16th mountain division, started. We would patrol with them, introducing them to the locals, the FOB and the difference in the ground throughout the AO. Then it was time, to say goodbye to Kandahar Air Base, a place I called home for 4.5 months.

Almost time, I looked out into the vast area around Kandahar, put a cigar in my mouth, lit it up, puffed out a big plume of smoke, took a big sigh of relief.

That's it, it's done, no one hurt, we did our job and did it well.

Next stop, Cyprus, time to decompress and have a well earned beer.

What would happen when I got home would change my life forever.

Welcome To Fatherhood Part 1

Walking through the hangers once again, and there was Katie, and the bump. I couldn't hide my joy, seeing the woman I love, with my unborn child, I almost burst into tears there and then, I gave Katie a kiss that was 4.5 months in the making. I then dropped to my knees and kiss the bump, my beautiful unborn daughter.

"Daddies home baby, daddies home"

I missed so much of the build, I left to go to Afghanistan and virtually no sign, I come home and there is a huge bump. I was ecstatic to be home, but fuck, I was so nervous. Would I make a good father? a good role model? Teacher? Protector? Etc.

Then the normal, what if she comes out and she's not healthy, underlining problems?

I knew she would be perfect. I new I'd love her unconditionally. The due date was creeping up fast, Katie was becoming more irritable but there was no sign of our little angel making an appearance. Due date came and went, followed by another week, still we waited. And waited and waited. 14 days late.

On the 28th June 2011, Katie went into Maidstone hospital, with some discomfort but no real signs. I wasn't aloud to stay with Katie overnight, which she hated when I went back to the in-laws, but we were in constant communications. And then finally at 05:00 I got that call from Katie, and I rushed to the hospital…. Still no sign though.

Hours flew by, and the signs started, but Katie was in a lot of discomfort, the Nurses checked her over and checked her temperature. "she's running hot, think we need to give her something for this fever she has?" The nurse administered some antibiotic's to Katie to reduce the fever. Few hours later they checked Katie again, no change, strange? The nurse then checked the thermometer, which was found to be broken, they pumped Katie and now the baby with antibiotics that they didn't need, I was fuming, but kept my cool for Katie.

"I need to push……." Said Kate

"You can't you are nowhere near ready" replied the nurse

"I need to push... I feel ready... I need to" Katie said more urgently

The nurse looked down, followed by "Oh... shall we have a baby"

At 18:20 on the 29th June 2011, out she came, all 6lbs 11oz of her, but it wasn't without a scare, for 45 seconds that seemed a life time, she wasn't breathing. Then the joy, that first cry, as the nurses brought her over, I couldn't control my self, the tears rolled down my cheeks as I saw and held my daughter for the first time. She was perfect.

"Just so you know Miss Stannard and Mr Thompson, your baby girl needs to finish the course of antibiotics…. Does baby girl have a name?" Asked the Nurse

I turned to Katie, and smiled the only name we both agreed on.

"Jessica"

My little " Sprogly" so small, so innocent so perfect. I never felt a love like it. A daughter's first love is her Father. And I wouldn't change her for the world. She's now growing up into an amazing young woman, intelligent, funny, sassy and the kindest soul.

We lost a huge part during my 3rd tour of duty, bath time was always our thing, playing Ed Sheeran loud as we splashed about, we lost a lot of time, and the connection wasn't there. In time it would grow, and the connection grew and grew. We were best buddies again, watching TV series together, smiling laughing and celebrating.

I couldn't be prouder of the woman she's turning into. Her kind heart and how sensitive she really is, stands out. She was even there for me in my darkest hour.

From The Desert To The Aisle

After the birth of Jessica, we were in the buildup to our wedding day. For the past four months, Katie had it all in hand, with pretty much little to no input from me. Throughout my tour of Afghanistan, all I could think about was Katie and Jessica as well as becoming a proper family. For my input it was simple, two best men and eight Guards of Honour.

Clearly, the most important part, the STAG DO… But from the moment I laid eyes on Katie I knew new, I played it down the best I could. Kept it close to my chest, but when you know you know, meeting her parents and family, I knew I wanted to be apart of this. Wives, Fiancé's and Girlfriends don't get enough credit for what they put up with, in regards to the mental pressure they go through. Katie had to endure not only Iraq with me, but also through pregnancy and planning a wedding. What she is made up of, they need to bottle so many emotions.

The night before, both sides of the families met some for the first time. Katie seemed nervous and as for me.... Well nothing what a few drinks won't cure, have a couple of beers, couple of whiskeys, and a nice toast with the gunners and my cousin of port.

Could I sleep...... could I fuck, exited nervous, seeing Katie in her dress, the wedding breakfast, and my speech (I didn't write in the end, thought making it up on the spot would be more organic and heart felt) Knock at the door....

"Morning mate, you ready!?!" Came the voice which belonged to my brother Darren through a fog of drunken sleep, he was always there to get me up going. Safe to say, with a slight hangover and now officially a bag of nerves, unable to eat my McDonald's breakfast. Then it was time to get my number one uniform on, medals shined, buckles polished, and boots ready.

Arriving at the church, waiting with the lads, pacing, chatting with family and friends, more pacing checking my watch, more pacing, looking around and realising I don't have any ushers....

"Where the fuck are Katies brothers." I thought whilst waiting. In typical Stannard fashion, late....always late. In my head, I was suddenly thinking "Now does that mean Katie's going to be late? Is she coming?...Has she chinned me off?

"Tommo.........She's here" Came the voice. Every emotion was racing through me. Relief, the stress of this morning and the build up, everything we have been through, that weight was lifted from my shoulders, a sense of calm came over me, then the wedding march began to play.

I turned to see Katie walking down the isle arm in arm with her dad. In a beautiful ivory dress, absolutely stunning. It was one of the best days of my life. The speeches from my two best friends, my brother Darren and Nick. And finally being married

to my soul mate, the woman of my dreams.

Herrick 17:

A Tour To End All Tours

This was going to be my final tour, my last goodbye. A final stand. I made the decision to leave, at the time, having a wife and daughter as well as the buildup to deploy, the idea of leaving was hard. Katie was struggling leaving her family, and the stress of me whilst on exercise, pre-deployment and the thought of me going away again (even though I was "safe on HQ flight") was beginning to take a toll on us as partnership, becoming more distant. I knew what I had to do and that was to take the step I never thought I would take and leave the job I wanted to do from a child, my dream. But what was more important... my job or my family?

Easy for me, family first always. I stood, Katie with tears in her eyes, and Jessica in the pushchair looking up at her Daddy with no idea what was about to happen, I held Kate tight, not wanting to let go, fighting back my tears one final kiss goodbye. I knelt to my beautiful baby daughter "Be good for your mummy, daddy will be home soon. I love you" I held her one last time before turning and heading towards the coach for the 3rd and final trip to RAF Brize Norton.

Being the lead signaller on the Squadron, for me meant one thing, treat yourself to every major incident to happen on 15 Squadron, and two that would change me as a person later in life. On the plane out I kept thinking "Thank fuck this was my last tour" but 3 tours in, 5 years isn't something to be ashamed of. This time was Bastian, located in

Helmand Province Afghanistan. As always, we spent the opening weeks acclimatising to the shit!

Nights were still the hardest part, looking up at my bunk, just thinking about home, my wife and child home. I was part of the HQ Flight now, J6 (comms ops) and I spent my days in the command centre (CJOC). My work space instead of my previous tours that was spent being out on the ground, in the cold desert nights. I was in a boarded up communications room, the hub of our area of operations. Crawling with high ranking officers, SNCO's, foreign nationals and the mighty USMC.

My mornings walking into the CJOC, I would be greeted by a powerful shout from the Marines "GOOD MORNING WAR FIGHTER"

"Jesus Christ mate I haven't even had a coffee yet" I thought.

Coming into month 3 of my tour, early December 2012, the day started like any other normal day. Spent it giving the USMC shit about movies like Jarhead, what I didn't know it was about to become extremely chaotic in the CJOC.

"HELLO GRANITE 0 THIS IS GRANITE 91C CONTACT WAIT OUT" came the comms through the speaker

Immediately the CJOC erupted into FLAP CON 2, the sniper section are in a contact. I take a second and remained calm as possible, thinking to my self "Tommo mate, this is what you've trained for" You must keep everything precise and to the point, and make sure the C/S knows that they have the support "Granite 91C this is Granite 0, Air support is available if required and QRF inbound" What I wasn't expecting, it was about to get much, much worse.

"HELLO GRANITE 0 THIS IS GRANITE 91C, MAN DOWN MAN DOWN, MAN DOWN, STAND BY FOR 9 LINER"

You train but you don't expect this to happen. "FUCK" no matter what pin comes over the net... its going to be a friend. Having to assist in the coordination between the Quick Reaction Force (QRF) the Sniper section, and the air desk to get the med evac sorted.

What you don't need whilst under immense pressure of getting as much information from the ground as possible and passing it to the relevant C/S , is a radio check from a SGT out on the ground, nothing to do with the Contact or QRF. "STAY OFF THE NET" what I wanted to say was "GET OFF MY NET YOU MASSIVE THUNDER CUNT WE HAVE TROOPS IN CONTACT AND A CASUALTY, GET A GRIP AND START SPARKING" Thankfully the coordination of the med-evac went smoothly, and PEDRO (US special forces medics) got him out of there, luckily it was only a ricochet that hit under the body armour.

Patched up and sent home.

"Tommo? You alright son?" Came the voice out of nowhere. "All good, you mind if I take a minute?" I replied. I took a minute to settle my head, have a coffee, and get back into the hot seat.

Yet again, I'm stood, seeing in the New Year in the desert, lighting my cigar, blowing the smoke out into the star lit sky. The year is now 2013, my last year in the military!

Throughout this tour, I began to question a lot about what was going on within Afghanistan itself. I used to just take orders and do as a good Gunner should, shut up and do. But when you take a moment to think about what is going on, why the locals turn to the Taliban, can't be surprised when armoured vehicles ploughing through their crops, breaking into their compound and constantly detaining and questioning locals. If that happened here you definitely would get your back up, maybe not as extreme as IEDs and Rockets but that's what they know. Certain things really stick in your head, watching from the view of an aircraft after intel was passed about IEDs being placed, AIR STRIKE was permitted and a confirmed kill of the "insurgent" placing the IED. Celebrations "HOORAH, KILL" was bellowed around the CJOC from the USMC. More intel was received from the troops on the ground. The "insurgent" was a 12 year old girl, brainwashed by the Taliban to place the IED.

"Hello Granite 0 this is Granite 20B, CONTACT IED WAIT OUT!!!"

The words no signaller wants to hear. The adrenaline hits you and your heart races faster and faster, trying to focus and get all relative forms ready, trying not to flap, to stay calm, the sweat pouring from your head, thinking the worst. "Calm the fuck down Tommo" I'd say to myself, trying to get a grip of the situation, "Mate its harder for them, remember you are in the CJOC they're on the ground, sort it out"

THEN IT GETS WORSE!

"Hello Granite 0 this is Granite 20B, 9 liner" The CAS report coming in 3x Casualty, 1 CAT A double amputee both legs, soon as the pin was read out, my heart sank, a close friend, someone I had been on the two previous tours with, played football and rugby with, active, married, father and now has life changing injures. Watchkeeper and the Air desk were given the information, and other C/S on the ground got the information. TRICKY (MERT British casualty evac team) my friend, now on route to the UK, now legless.

I sat in my chair, put my headset down, and just put my hands on my head. I looked up at the roof, unable to process my emotions. My hands shaking in the shock of the injuries sustained to my friend. I hoped they had got him home, safe, and alive. "Tommo, he's your mate, he's on his way home, you did amazing work, he will be fine. Go take a break" came the voice. I stepped outside, walked to bathroom, splashed some water on my face to snap me out of the daze. Then I broke down, on my own, only for a few seconds, I wiped the tears, looked at myself in the mirror "MAN up Tommo. You're the signaller, stop being weak".

CPL Stuart "Robbo" Robinson lost both his legs whilst on a routine patrol at Camp Bastion, Helmand

Province. He would go onto make the most of his injuries, medalling in the INVICTUS games, and joining Team GB to play in the Paralympics in wheelchair rugby.

Life as a signaller always had its ups and downs, most of the time it was shit banter from the lads on the ground, but time to time you would get shit from a SNCO, one stands out more than most. A Flight Sergeant on HQ J2 int cell, he would cut about saying how unprofessional I was. This coming from the same SNCO that I personally handed int from the ground

- 4x IED Teams
- 4x Insurgent KIA after air strike from the USMC

- 1x 12 year old minor killed

None of this information was passed out on the ground through the daily down report, information that was important and vital for the men on the ground. And I was called unprofessional, for occasionally sending some moral over the net such as the football results. Coming towards the end of the tour, 2 Sqn and 3 Sqn were there to take over, but not before OP CENTURION DAGGER, which took place on 20th April 2013, 0746L again in the hot seat,

"Hello Granite 0, Contact wait out" This time it was expected, but still the thought of rounds pinging around the lads on the ground and you're stuck, unable to help, accept from passing on the information. It's hard training so long to be an infantry solider and when it's time to use it, you're sat in a chair listening and watching others get the action. Jealous, but I gave a zealous account of myself over the net. The multiple expended 184 rounds, including,

- .50mm
- 338mm

But the main attack happening from the coordination of the JTACs on the ground, which called in Air Support from the Apache's which were on station. Which in turn expended :

- 400 x .50mm
- 750 x 7.62mm
- 250 x 20mm

Number of insurgents killed was x2. Bit overkill really for 2 insurgents but still a win for the Squadron.

As the wind blew hard, I struggled to light my cigar, soon I would be flying home, huge deep breath as I inhaled the smoke from my cigar and swirled it around my mouth before exhaling. So many emotions I had bottled up inside, every major incident I have been part of including the injuries involving two close friends, the rocket attacks on the camp, the deliberate OP, and the poor 12 year old girl who was brainwashed and lost her life. I haven't spoke about the stresses I had over there because I thought it was nothing compared to the guys and girls on the ground. And the up and coming pressure of leaving my dream behind, handing in my kit, my rifle, my mark one issue friends. I felt as though I was loosing a lot and I was petrified. I had negative thoughts clouding my mind and the fear of failure dragging me down.

So I decided to write it down;

"Dear Failure, what if I told you the sacrifices I made to compete are victory in itself? What if I did not measure my success by wins and loses, but my will, my triumph over slumber, my focus to prepare and my courage to contend. What if I told you I win every morning when my eyes open. Failure you will not triumph over me because I am possible." Unknown

Now it's time to leave the desert, start a fresh. Part of me will always be in the military will always be a Gunner. For I am still in the desert.

Welcome To Fatherhood Part 2

This time I was around. Every scan, every kick, every moment. During the build up, it was also the process of me leaving the Military. We moved into the in laws house. 3 of us, soon to be 4 living in a room. This wouldn't last for long before we began to get under each others feet. I was exited to be involved in every minor detail this time. However cracks were beginning to form within myself. I suppressed these thoughts and feelings the best I could, I had to be strong especially with the latest edition getting closer to coming into the world.

Edging closer and I could see Katie becoming more and more uncomfortable. Even getting calls at work to get home because she felt symptoms of labour. We would take practice trips to Pembury hospital, getting the timings right.

05:00 on the 25th of February 2014, the labour began. At 06:20, Katie finally woke me up, she was in a lot of pain. "Oh shit don't panic don't panic, where's the go bag, where's the fucking go bag?" I started to think, trying not to flap, but flapping was what I was doing. Seeing the woman you love in pain and not able to actually do anything, will bring any man to his knees with anxiety going through the roof.

07:00 came around, leaving plenty of time….. so we thought, hitting every red light possible, bin-men and at points, Katie yelling at me to jump the lights and just get there.

"I'm trying to not kill us all." I tried explained, "Just hurry up!!!!!" Katie said whilst grimacing in pain. At 08:22, we arrived at Pembury Hospital, in our rush we had forgotten the car seat. Katie was moved to the ward and into a room swift and sharp.

"I just need the toilet" Katie said in pain…….. "Nope I need to push" "Has the waters gone yet"……POP! The waters shot across the room. I stood, pretty much out of the way like a lemon unable to really do or help in any way until. "She's here" as the head and shoulders came out there she was, my beautiful baby girl.

At 08:45 and weighing in at 8lbs 8oz, Sophia Harriet Rose Thompson was born, full thick black hair, I cut the cord, swaddled her up and held her tight. Perfect, simply perfect, even after the birth of Jessica. It still doesn't prepare you for the overwhelming emotion that comes over you. Our beautiful baby girl. She would grow up to be so smart, so beautiful, huge blue eyes, fine blonde hair. Full of Sass, and a temper like her Dad. In an imperfect world, I had managed to bring up not one but two, respectful polite, beautiful amazing young ladies. With all the problems I ended up having, both Jessica and Sophia helped me through my darkest of times.

In the wake

Leaving the military was one of the toughest decisions I had to make, it wasn't something I took lightly, it wasn't just an off the cuff moment like "fuck it 7 clicks time to go" I fell out of love with the job I wanted to do since I was a child. A job that was a dream, a job that was supposed to be my career for life, following in the foot steps of my Father and Grandfather, both serving full terms and then some. But for me, my time was up. I had done 3 tours of duty and at the time I thought I was mentally sound. "Do you miss it?!" Is a question I get asked all the time, it's a complex question, there are many aspects I miss. Would I sign up again if needed? I don't think there's a veteran out there that wouldn't.

I went through a very limited resettlement, which in truth didn't give me any guidance to life as a civilian. I took on a Close Protection and surveillance course thinking it was the most suited to me, not thinking about life as a civilian, qualifications needed and how to do anything really. Basically shown the door "Ciao have a good one kid". I suppose what hurt the most was the lack of goodbye from the squadron, no leaving do, no leaving gift, fuck all. Even lads who moved squadrons and that had only been there 5 minutes got something. I'd been their 5 years including 3 tours and nothing, still bugs me today.

For me it was now simple, I had to provide for my family. I am a husband, a father with one more on the way, you can't sit and feel sorry for yourself or show any regrets, this was my decision now, man up and crack the fuck on. Easier said than done, on the outside I seemed pretty normal, my grumpy sarcastic self, but what was happening inside was starting to take hold.

After becoming a dad for the second time, life took a whole new meaning. There was another beautiful angel that needed me. My role as a protector and provider had now doubled.

I found getting a job pretty easy, straight into the over saturated, under qualified security industry. I took to it well but something didn't feel right, I was restless, anxious, bitter and angry all the time, the negative self loathing and lack of self worth started to bring me down. It dragged me to the bottom and tormented me to thinking I was nothing but a joke, a fool and a laughing stock.

"You're a security officer mate, you used to wear the uniform, medals on your chest, now look at you, a pitiful shell of a man that once was something important" screamed the voices in my head. Those thoughts of endless negativity would poison my mind each day, making it harder for me to sleep, concentrate, consuming all my focus, making me pour another glass of whiskey. Making wrong decisions at work, getting disciplinary's at work, the spiral would then take form into more anger and more drink.

I became restless at work needing new a scenery, and then I'd bounce to a new job, and again and again. All the while being told you have a problem. Rage would strike from nowhere, shouting loudly, throwing toys and scaring the girls. This was a constant cycle. All forming from the lack of self purpose. And the negative anguish I placed on myself.

I felt as though I was letting everyone down, I was a disappointment to my family when I left the military, and now I scare my children and wife. I felt like an embarrassment to be feeling so down, I was so angry all the time, but also had no idea what was going on inside my head.

I found myself bouncing from job to job, unable to settle, soon as I started I would be fine, within a few weeks my feet would begin to get itchy, people would begin to get to me. My level of frustration within myself would rise, unable to understand what was going on within me. I thought it was the job. So I'd change job. And change job and change job and still I wouldn't feel complete, missing something and further down I would go without accepting it or talking about it. Along with Katie, and a long hard think I took the opportunity to talk to a therapist. Soon as I sat on the sofa, I could feel my emotions building up.

"Let's start from the beginning" I was asked, as soon as the words started coming out of my mouth like an emotional flood, so did the tears. Going through things I saw as a child, and things I had dealt with within my tours of duty. Which I took as 'Just part of the job' not believing I could suffer because I wasn't in a Rambo movie, or seen action anywhere near the other units. I had never opened myself up like that before, a rush of emotions, tears truth and a long look deep inside.

My arrogance would cost me, I went to therapy for a couple of weeks, more and more would come out, the Doctor diagnosed me with PTSD. I still didn't believe it and after those few weeks I thought I was 'Better' so I stopped going.

I left another job, that being the fifth in as many years, still struggling to settle, and finding myself still loosing my temper. Parking up my work vehicle and crying on my own, feeling pathetic, low, negative thoughts blacking out my mind. I felt useless, unloved, no self esteem. On the outside I was 'fine' on the inside I was crying out for help, guidance, something to get me on the path. I felt so alone, the darkness eating me alive, and starting to effect not just me, but the ones around me, I was SO angry at myself, for being like this. Looking back from the position I am in now, could more be done? with more and more former service personnel going down with Depression, Anxiety, PTSD and worst case Suicide. I believe more needs and should be done to develop the tools in guidance for veterans and serving members.

Surveillance

I arrived in Gloucester, ready to start training to become a Surveillance Operative. Could I have found a job where I was finally happy? It was tough, basically becoming a spy for insurance companies, following those that claim big, and from what I found during my time, most that claim big are liars. Over the 2 week course, we learnt how to hide in plain sight, whether on foot or in a vehicle, tactics that we learned on following was eye opening, I used to think "How many people are in their own world, not paying any attention to their surroundings?" It makes it easier to hide, record and log exactly what the subject is doing.

I was hooked from the start (unfortunately like most my jobs, that was short lived) Some days were a slog, mentally, no movement and no action, 8 hours in the back of a van, either freezing or melting, pissing into a bottle as well as trying to remain focused. Others are what you signed up for. The big fish are the ones you know you will get a huge pat on the back for.

Subject X - unable to walk more than 100m, unable to lift heavy objects, unable to stand for long periods.

"Stand by, Stand By, Subject out and into Subject Vehicle, in as driver, minors into SV as passengers, reversing, and off off off" The voice explained.

We followed the SV for miles and miles until we were told "Stop, stop, stop. SV now static in car park of Thorpe Park, Subject out of SV, lifting minor above head and onto shoulders, now walking towards

entrance to Thorpe park approx 200m away"

In theory we could have stopped him, we had him

bang to rights, but to make sure, we got both our

cameras and covert cameras and followed him for a

further 5 hours around Thorpe Park, constantly

gathering the evidence. The more we got, the sweeter

the taste.

SUBJECT Y – Unable to walk, wheel chair bound,

Medical day.

These were the best days, catching them before the

medical, during and after, we could see the full

spectrum of how much these people big up their claims and how, most the time it's total fabrication.

I set up shop at the medical location, firmly positioned in a prime place looking at the parking lot and the main door of the medical centre.

I had already received information from my partner that she walked to the car from the house (already a win) now I was sitting and waiting.

"Contact contact, SV now reversing into space, that's F1 out of the vehicle round to the boot, takes out wheel chair, walk to the passenger side opens door, SUBJECT out, helped into wheel chair by F1, F1 pushes SUBJECT to the stairs, where she shakenly moves up the stairs and IN IN to medical".

I tried to keep my cool and not laugh at such ridiculousness, the same on the way out of the medical. We followed the Subject out of London to a services where I got out and followed her in. The Subject walked from the vehicle, approx 150m, then around the services stopping for a coffee, I was smug, capturing all of this on my covert camera, I was living the dream. Finally a sense of pride in what I was doing. Another one banged to rights.

SUBJECT Z - unable to walk long distances, unable to lift objects,

Not all jobs go to plan.

This job started off swimmingly, we got the subject out, and into a gym. Sometimes when this happens, things can go pear shaped especially when you get arrogant with it. Under the guidance of the team leader I went into the Gym as I 'would fit in more' so I did, signed up to the gym under a false name, I was shown around the gym and got a fair bit of footage, even a free taster session which I took advantage of. Getting as much footage as I could, I began to get a bit over confident with my filming, and a bit zealous with the amount I had captured. I positioned myself with my back to the Subject, camera on. I continued the 'work out'

"Are you filming me?!!" Asked the Subject, I quickly fired back with "Pardon what you on about?!" "Your filming me, I'm getting security and the police on this" They replied, obviously pissed off with the situation they had found themselves in. I showed no emotion and simply replied "Do what you like I'm finished now anyway"

Then the subjects parents come storming over, followed by a torrent of questions "Who do you think you are? Filming my daughter, who are you?!? What are you filming ? Show me" They demanded. I had to play it cool, even though I had nearly blown my cover, I fell straight into my cover story. "Firstly, my name is James (fake name) secondly, I'm trying to work out, do you want to see my phone? Enjoy" I

said as I showed them my work phone, nothing on it!
I shoved the covert one away until it was hidden, then
I hid in the changing room for a few minutes before
legging it.

It can't all go your way, I found myself being in court
a few times filming near parks, which the police were
almost called. As I was smashed through the days, the
months, the love and the excitement was beginning to
fade I was positioned in places, miles from where I
should be and for very little action. I saw little
progression in the job, only to move from a van to a
car, and those that's face fitted, going up the ladder
quicker.

The isolation and the amount of time on my own,
with the darkness of my own thoughts, was beginning
to take control of me.

My moods where shifting. The smallest of things
starting to irritate again! And my temper was off the
scale, I had to do something. But where to start! Do I
quit or do I seek help. In the end it was both!!

Discovering Sean

"Take a seat Mr Thompson" I was asked. I sat, nervous already, I was fidgeting, my palms sweating, a huge knot in my stomach that I have never had before. Why was I feeling like this, it was though I was a kid again going home to explain to my dad that I had been suspended.

"Relax Sean, this is a safe place, there is no judgment here" I was told. I took a long deep breath.

"Let's start at the beginning" came the usual request.

The rush of emotion came pouring out of me, and was an endless flood of thoughts feelings, loss, pain, sadness, disappointment, regrets. All these emotions I had been storing away inside for years, from before the military from child hood. Things that I wish I

hadn't seen or heard. Things that for now are

between me and my wife and therapist. Reasons to

why I am, the need to impress others to feel like I

mattered, the lack of self belief, pride and

confidence. Not dealing with the emotions of 3 tours

and the stresses, the losses of 3 unborn

children. Leaving my dream job and the idea of

having such pride in what I stood for.

I was a lost soul, with a negative undertone that was

taking over me and my life, pushing those away that

care for me that loved me.

I was my own worst enemy! I looked in the mirror

and didn't seen myself anymore. I saw nothing but

disappointment and a let down. It was killing me. In that mirrored image was a face, no smile, teardrops falling down the cheeks, "This wasn't Tommo, this wasn't Sean, who is this guy?" I asked myself as I starred at myself. I didn't know myself any more and the more I fought, the more I was suffocating.

I lasted a few sessions in therapy, each time scratching away at the surface, each time I sat and cried to a complete stranger, who knew there was more to this.

I stopped the sessions, I was fixed or so I thought, I was wrong.

But there was a long journey still ahead, I didn't know the turn I was about to face within myself, I put up barriers and walls that were weak, flimsy, easily chipped away and broken. At this moment I wore a smile, I kept everything and everyone at arms length hiding behind fake smiles and laughter.

Sean was in there somewhere, discovering him again was proving to be a difficult task. For so many years I would say I was dark and dead inside, each time putting a nail into the coffin of Sean. But I'm not dead, I was very much alive. Doors were unlocked to Pandora's box, doors that should have been dealt with and not just left open, the monster was creeping out to take me down, again and again, time after time.

The Darkening

My 5th job in as many years! I was beginning to see that I had a problem.

I couldn't seem to settle, I wasn't part of a team. What I was doing was making me feel unfulfilled and monotonous. I was a security officer, like the ones people make fun of on TV. Plastic police, pointless and most of the time, fat and lazy. Anyone with half a brain could do this job. And before I knew it, the darkness would strike again.

At 04:30 my alarm would go off, on the bike in the ice cold rain as it hit me in the face, as I struggled to make my way to work. I would be isolated most the day, just me and my over powering negative thoughts. Bringing me down to my knees. I would

look in the rearview mirror at myself and just be
disappointed, feeling like I had let down the
family. Pulling off my clip on tie, the rain pouring
down on the security vehicle, as the tears rolled down
my face.

I felt alone, trapped in my own mind. The more I
fought, the weaker I became. The fake smile would
only last so long, as cracks began to form. Each day I
would say "I'm fine, I'm good, tip top" Inside I was
screaming out "HELP ME"

I hid away from my friends laughing off the thought
of being depressed or having PTSD. Inside I was
petrified of appearing weak, scared to admit the scars
that were formed were reopening and taking over.

I was in a dark place, the more I was alone, the darker it became, the more tears I cried and the more I pushed away those people closest to me!

I couldn't cope with this version of myself, I hated who I have become! The depression had fully taken hold of me, and I was being consumed by it, there was little left of me, Sean inside, just a black hole of nothing, I was numb. My dream died years ago and I hadn't let go, I hadn't mourned the fact I was no longer a Gunner, just a civilian now, and the lack of pride and self belief had taken over and left me in tears. I hated myself for what I had become, and I took out my anger and frustration on those closest to me.

I needed a way! I needed something, a glimmer of light to spark the beacon to guide me back to being Sean. I was lost in the darkness of depression now, I needed to find my back.

Facing the Truth

I'm stronger than this, it can't happen to me I would think. As I found myself again silently crying to myself. I thought about it all "I have it all, a beautiful wife, 2 amazing daughters, my own house and a secure job" But still, the self negativity would take hold and drag me down into the depths of despair. Tears rolling down my cheeks, as the overwhelming sense of failure would take hold. No feeling like it, the feeling of worthlessness consumes you and makes you feel like you are not good enough.

But still the same thoughts run through my head "Dry your eyes mate, you will get through this, keep it locked inside, don't show weakness, you're a Soldier, you're stronger than this. What would the lads think if they knew. Now stop being a cunt and man up!" It was like a rollercoaster that would be continuously crashing out of control. The constant fight in my own mind would eventually take its toll.

I've never been to good at hiding my emotions, it's usually written all over my face, but still I managed to hide what was really going on inside, but this was a huge mistake, I know this now and I wish I could tell that Tommo to sort it out. I began to push away everyone close to me, my moods would change at a drop of a hat, I would shout and scream at the girls for nothing, I had no control. "I'm fine" was all I would say. The get out of jail card used far too much and so easy to say like a reflex, a reaction said without thought. I wasn't 'Fine' and on the 2nd of March 2019, when I was curled up in a ball on the floor of my kitchen with my eldest Jessica, wiping my tears from my eyes and telling me it was "OK to be sad" and " I will look after you daddy" really gave me the realisation that I had to do something I had to turn this around, I couldn't have my daughters worrying about me, I couldn't push away everyone that cares for me.

It knew it wasn't going to be easy, but nothing in life worth doing ever is. I had to fight back against the dark clouds that circled in my mind. But it was time to take the first steps which are always the hardest and actually admitting I had a problem.

This was always going to be difficult, previously I had tried to raise awareness for mental health by doing a number of challenges, just after the lose of a friend and former Regiment gunner had taken his own life. But once I started, I began to get trolled, almost a form of bulling done through the internet done by those that have no back bone to do it in person, this was my first taste of it and it wouldn't be the last.

On the 4th March 2019 was the first of many huge steps into my acceptance and then into recovery from depression and anxiety. I pulled over, took a deep breath and hit record, that day was Episode 1 of the Granite Zero Podcast. I opened up so much and it was though I had word diarrhea. I let out an almighty wave of emotion and let go of all the stress, hate, negativity, zero structure and zero filter, just raw and unedited, just me baring my heart and my soul out to the world.

I have never been so scared, but also relieved. I had finally found my voice, finally allowed to say what I wanted to say, finally able to let go, and finally allowed to tackle the problems inside, head on, no more bottling up or hiding away. The realisation that I'm not a worthless sack of shit, that people do love and care for me and want me to be, well me. Darkness is no longer a weakness, more of a motivation to become a better person and show people that it's "ok to not be ok" and that we should all take a moment to let it out and talk.

Granite Zero has become much more than an outlet for me, but is now a part of me. I look forward to hitting the record button, meeting and chatting with new like minded people. Will I be the next Rogan, I don't think so but fuck it I'm loving it! New guests, new opportunities, new passion.

Getting the opportunity to chat with elite athletes, directors, veterans, doctors, influencers, PT instructors, psychologists helps broaden the mind. I've learned more about how everybody is unique, every body's mind is different. How people see and feel as well as understand situations are all as different as snowflakes and finger prints. Learning and understanding through other peoples outlooks and perspectives, and help guide people through their own dark places. This helps to bring peace to my own dark mind, we will heal and grow together as one team, through one effort.

BE MY GUEST

From episode One, I was always on my own. Recording 45 minutes plus the time spent on my own going over the thoughts, feelings and emotions. But there was only so much that I could grasp and articulate on my own, I needed someone to bounce off, someone to talk to. Not just in terms of mental health, but just general chat, it helps stimulate the mind and build networks, bonds outside of the normal day to day friends. It was time to invite some guests on the show.

A strange feeling would come over me, a nervousness that I hadn't felt in ages, alongside a new anxious feeling. A feeling similar to what I would get before a big sports match, or going out on patrol. A feeling of what if I 'fuck up' or "what if it's shit?" Or "what if

I'm shit?" This is a battle that would happen each time I hit record, even with close friends and family.

I have had some amazing guests from all walks of life.

"Welcome To The Granite Zero Podcast"

Adam DeRito was an outstanding guest, ones who's own story deserves it's own book. For hours we delved into his story of 'sexual harassment' within the military. Having Adam on the show helped spread his message, not only in the USA but also now in the UK. Where I know there will be others going through the same or similar situations, that interview could give them the courage to stand up and say their story as well.

Adam was sexually assaulted, black mailed, investigated, coerced into being an informant, and had his medical records falsified to make him seem mentally unstable, this was all done by the US Armed Forces.

"After we done our requests and done some information digging, only the past few weeks we finally got an answer back, there are no records that I was investigated by any civilian authority ever in the Colorado Springs Police Department. That potentially means that I was coerced and forcefully recruited into being an undercover informant for the Air Force office of Special Investigations against my will, being blackmailed into working for them, thinking I had

done something wrong when I hadn't and at 19 years old I didn't know any better"

(Extract from Episode 74, Adam DiRto, Granite Zero podcast)

The Podcast really did broaden my mind and out look on many different aspects of the world life and people. Talking to people with stories that are out of this world and how they cope and grow.

Shar Weil who also hosts a podcast called 'Blonde and Strong' has another amazing story that I was privileged enough to sit and chat with and hear the story first hand.

"When I was 17, I had a seizure I'd never had one before. By 18 I was diagnosed with an inoperable brain tumour, they told me they didn't know how long it had

been there, they didn't know how long it would take to kill me, whether it was benign or malignant, and because of where it was they couldn't operate. They would leave it, so it was bad enough that it would kill me, then they would test it to see if there was anything they could do. They believed it to be a slow growing tumour"

(Extract from Episode 69, Shar Weil, Granite Zero podcast)

To go along side these amazing stories I also have been able to sit and chat with some Elite athletes from the world of Mixed Martial Art, and one particular who has been on the show a handful of times, very humble, down to earth and an absolute machine and killer in the best of ways in the cage.

Mason "The Dragon" Jones, who when I first spoke to was a humble title challenger in the premium European organisation Cage Warriors, each time he came onto the show, a new notch on his belt, from contender, to champion to double champion to being signed to the world famous Ultimate Fighting Championship. But each time on the show the same Mason, from humble beginnings to world champion no change, and still an honour to call him a friend.

"Fighting is so natural to me, the hardest part is staying calm, it's not the fear I never worry, all the prep is done and to stay as calm as possible. Normally my dad stays with me in the coaching room, until I make my walk, then he runs to the stands and meets with me mam. This was the first time my dad wasn't

aloud in the coaching room, so it was just me and the coaches, one of my coaches is a bit of a stress head he worries about everything, the other two are the most laid back dudes you would ever meet in your life, we warmed up then made the walk, the only difference in the fight was I could hear my coaches more clearly and I could hear his coaches, a lot more clearly. With the crowd sometimes something funny can be heard, but most of the time you focus on the coaching team… you could hear the punches and kicks…..

The more mobile force will always win, that's the same with fighting, the faster than you and controlling distance and movement controlling the range there going to win. If you can stop them moving and can control the range, your in and strike and out not to get hit, you will win. And that's how I beat Joe, I slowed him down, and when he couldn't move so much I

pressed him against the cage and when I closed I knew

the knew was coming and that's what shut him down".

(Extract from Episode 61, Mason Jones on the Granite Zero Podcast)

I learned a lot from all my guests, each one as unique
as the next, but I really learned the most talking to
pro athletes, how they train not only their body to be
physically ready but also their minds, the athletes
mindset is one that can be taken deep into the dark,
how they withstand unbelievable utopian highs to at
some point the unrelatable lows. Fighters are at the
forefront of this, as most know fighters go into a
training camp surrounded by coaches and "team
mates" but in reality it's the individual that needs to
withstand the pressure, it's the fighter on his own
that really has to deal with the fight itself and the

outcome. Amazing and everyone loves you when you win, but where are these people if you lose.

I felt the same way in terms of my military career and my own mental health. All praising you calling you a "Hero" and "Thank you for your service" but when the uniforms gone and you are just left with the anger and hate and nothing but negative thoughts who's is there for you?

Which is why most servicemen and fighters will put up barriers and walls to prevent the closeness in the fear of losing more than once. I take pride in the fact that I have a very close relationship with my brother who has been a guest on the podcast the most, since the very beginning and has always been in high praise of the show and of me from the start. Although we have amazing banter and are extremely silly at times, we never shy away from hard hitting topics or how we feel inside. Its always an honour and forever my privilege to have him on my show. He's much more than my brother he's one of my best friends.

"What you're saying to me there, I'm going "Fuck that, it was hard enough me getting a message from my mate about Sue that works in Weatherspoon's, it's not somebody I deal with daily or that I know is in a dangerous position, that's awful…" and I'm there going "Give me any updates, anything you let me know. You're not in that position you have a fucking number come through, you go through the numbers and go that's my mate!!!!... he's fucked what can I

*do?" "Ohh fucking hell I got to send a chopper…
everybody has to do their job, if they don't someone is
fucked"*

*"That's what people don't understand, and from what I
read from the different trolls that you had entity, it was
unnecessary, the whole time I've been involved in this,
that's the first time I've heard you talk about that sort
of stuff and it makes me go "Oh that's fucked. Its fine
if you are depressed, anxiety etc but for someone to call
you out on having PTSD when you served with them, I
mean when I heard you talking about it, it literally
stressed me out, I had to make jokes because I could
cope with the stress of what you where telling me and it
wasn't even happening. Let alone actually being there*

and dealing with it, I can see you getting nervous

talking about it now"

(Extract from Episode 35, Remembrance with Darren Thompson on the Granite Zero Podcast)

Becoming Zero

I was now on the long journey that would see me go through peaks and troughs. Still taking anti-depressants, relying on tiny white tablets to control and balance my moods. I was no longer on ultimate highs and indescribable lows, with anger at the forefront in the driving seat of my moods.

I was numb. Balanced in mood, but numb.

Just a shell, with a man inside that didn't really know what do with himself. The podcast had hit new highs for me, new guests each week, new people to chat, new stories to tell and share, but something wasn't right. Steps needed to be taken to aid in the recovery. The first steps had already happened with the podcast, talking to the doctor and actually communicating with Katie about how I'm feeling inside.

I started with a few online courses to help broaden the outlook on mental health. One that stood out for me was 'Depression Awareness and Life Coaching' This not only helped guide me but to help and assist others in similar positions as myself.

The best thing I ever did was get involved in a project call INNER ARMOUR. Breath taking coaching that uses Positive Psychology and post traumatic growth. I took a huge leap of faith. Without the advice of the doctor I stopped my anti-depressants, I had a huge about of faith in this course I was about to join.

We all met at the hotel, grabbed a beer and all sat in and around the bar. 10 of us from different walks of

life, but all had similarities in common. There were
former commissioned officers in the British Army
and Royal Marines, JNCOs from the RAF Regiment
and Royal Marines, a former head of counter
terrorism in the Met Police, and myself, a former
RAF Regiment gunner (no rank) and a guy who gobs
off on a podcast for fun. I didn't feel comfortable, felt
slightly embarrassed to be in the room with such
distinguished soldiers and marines, holding high
ranks, awards like MBE's and one leading the
invasion of Iraq in 03. I hid in the comfort of my
phone and went into my shell.

The course started, and it was high intensity and dug
deep into the soul, searching into the darkness that
controlled each of us in different ways. We all opened

up, and unloaded our souls to the chief instructor,

taking into account what we had all been through,

and what each of us gives separately. We used the

techniques that were coached to us so we could help

each other. We listened, we guided and we coached.

But most importantly we grew, as a team and as

individuals learning more about ourselves and

understanding what goes on within our own minds, it

gave us the gift that we can now help number 1.

For me it was huge, these newfound skills I could use

when I found myself going down into the negative

darkness that was inside. But now I have the light,

the light I can take anywhere with me, safe in the

knowledge that if anything was to happen or take

hold, or I experience a period in my life where I'm at

a loss, or stuck, I can now firmly hold my head high and be confident that I can control my own fate.

After struggling for years, what seemed a lifetime, not knowing which version of myself was going to show up, I took those anti-depressants and threw them away. No longer did I need them to balance my mood, at the price of losing myself, being numb both mentally and physically. I was firmly in control, starting again from Zero, building myself back up. Life was becoming as it should be. I became happy.

"You know, everyone hates you right?"

"You're attention seeking"

"It's not just me that doesn't like it! Its pretty all of the regiment. You're making a mockery out of lads that have actually been through things!"

Some of the online hate that I got, since starting the podcast, it's hard at times when you are struggling with darkness and negativity in the mind to keep control of the emotions, and not spiral down into the depths of the shit. Before I got the help in needed I would get down, upset, angry and wanting to get revenge. But now I feel sorry for them. I think what could be going on in their lives is that they feel that bad, they have to bring someone down with them. Instead of being a candle and lighting the way for others to follow them out of the shit.

And the war is still going on. Little battles have been won.

A journey that started as a boy with a dream to be an Action Man, that same dream that took him to the desert, where part of him will always be. And now fighting through mental health, the fight that is ongoing in the mind, he picked himself up from Granite Zero, to winning the fight talking each week on a podcast. The journey is forever.

I was always taught to end on a quote

"A story. A man fires a rifle for many years. and he goes to war. And afterwards he comes home, and he sees that whatever else he may do with his life - build a house, love a woman, change his son's diaper - he will always remain a jarhead. And all the jarheads killing and dying, they will always be me. We are still in the desert.......

EVERY WAR IS DIFFERENT EVERY WAR IS THE SAME"

Anthony Swofford

This book is dedicated to

My Wife, my Rock without whom I wouldn't have made it through my darkest days

My Children, to whom I owe so much, and I give my all

My family, always in my corner

Those that stood by me helped me and guided me. To those that gave the ultimate sacrifice, we owe so much and they gave their all. For they gave their tomorrows so we can have our today. Lest we Forget

"To those that struggle, to those in the dark, use this book as a guiding light. We can make it through."

Sean Thompson 2020

Printed in Great Britain
by Amazon